JOHN WILLIAMS POETRY

For Children

Cyberwit.net
HIG 45 Kaushambi Kunj, Kalindipuram
Allahabad - 211011 (U.P.) India
http://www.cyberwit.net
Tel: +(91) 9415091004
E-mail: info@cyberwit.net

Printed at Thomson Press India Limited.

CONTENT

GROWING UP

I have a pup called Sheeba
And Muttley is her mate,
And when it comes to dinner time
My pups are never late.

They ate my Gargoyle monster set,
They ate my teddy bear,
They ate my pet goanna,
They just didn't seem to care.

They ate my budgie Hercules,
They ate my mother's mat,
Now they waddle everywhere,
My pups are very fat.

DOG AND HIS BONE

A dog with a bone was on the roam,
Where can I find this bone a home?
Will I bury it next to the tree?
No, too easy for others to see.

What about next to the garden shed?
Maybe in the middle of the garden bed,
Behind the sty where the pigs all are,
What about somewhere right away far.

I think I know what I will do,
I'll just sit down and have a chew,
Tomorrow is another day,
I'll find a spot then for the bone to stay.

MY PUPS

Litter sisters playing hard,
Romping round our big front yard,
"I will catch you soon sister dear,"
"No you won't I have no fear,
I'll swivel here, then dart around,
You'll be left laying on the ground,
You can't turn as fast as me,
Ha, ha, ha, I'm running free."

Little Muff dipped her rump,
Exploding legs caused her to jump,
Bindi rolled with Muff on top,
The game came to a grinding stop.

My doggies chase every day,
Until they're just too tired to play,
They come inside, rest their paws,
Get ready for the next doggie wars.

SssSnake

Sss went the snake
As he slithered from a log,
Uup went my hair
As I broke into a jog.

Hhhelp I yelled aloud
As I ran so very hard,
Sss went the snake
As he came into my yard.

Mmmeow went the cat
As he scurried up a tree,
Sss went the snake
As he bit a bumble bee.

Ggrrr went the dog
As he bit the snake in two,
Aaah! went the snake
As he yelled for the glue.

THE ALLIGATOR

One day I saw an alligator,
He said, "May I take a bite?
Your fingers look real juicy
And your legs will fill my appetite."

I said, "No way Al baby,
My fingers are so handy,
My legs I need for walking
In your swamp where it's so sandy."

I said, "What about you alligator
Can you do without your skin?
You see I want an alligator bag
To put my school things in."

He said, "You must be joking
My skin's a very vital part,
It keeps the mossies and the snakes
From acting far too smart."

After that we were good friends,
Sometimes around the swamp I ride,
Although my seat is very knobbly
Al makes a great swamp guide.

GORILLA IN THE KITCHEN

I don't know why she's done it,
She normally is quite sane,
Mum said she bought a new gorilla,
It really is a pain.

She said she put it in the kitchen
Not far from the sink,
What if I want to go to the tap
And get myself a drink.

I wonder how large it is?
If it will sit with us to eat?
I wonder what we'll name it?
And where it's going to sleep?

But when I tip-toed to the kitchen
A large animal I didn't see,
It was just an electric griller
And mum cooking lunch for me.

MISTY KITTEN

My name is Misty Kitten,
I like to chase my tail,
I've never caught it yet,
Each time I seem to fail.

I like to jump and pounce
And to box with my paw,
Then chase a ball of wool
Across a slippery floor.

I like to chase butterflies,
To go in hollow logs,
I like to climb trees
Then hiss at puppy dogs.

But most of all I think I like
To lay down with my mum,
To drink lots of milk
Then stretch out in the sun.

DETECTIVE SNOOPER

Detective Snooper is a bloodhound of note
He takes down details with a bone-coloured pen,
Then sets out to solve farmyard mysteries
He's done it time and again.

This morning he's down at the henhouse
His assistant Angus Duck stands just nearby,
Mrs. Hen is protesting, her chicks have gone missing,
Her wings in a flap she cries, "Why?"

"Don't worry Mrs. Hen we'll find your lost chicks,"
Snooper reassures his feathery friend,
With his nose to the ground the detective hound
Finds some tracks leading past the pig pen.

Angus was quacking, Snooper was sniffing,
Fox tracks were becoming quite clear,
Beyond the dense bush they could see curling smoke,
Foxy's den was dangerously near.

On top of the ridge they saw a bark shack,
The name M. T. Fox was on the front door,
So they devised a plan to lend the chicks a hand
These custodians of farmyard law.

Angus quietly approached and climbed the den roof,
Then blocked the chimney of billowing smoke,
Foxy began coughing, his eyes began hurting,
Snooper waited to catch this villainous bloke.

When the fox emerged Snooper pawed him and chopped him,
This felonious fiend was certainly no match,
For Snooper knew Dograti, the canine form of karate,
Foxy ran off through a thistle patch.

The crime-busting duo returned the lost chicks,
Angus celebrated with a feed of snail,
As Snooped gnawed a bone in the distance he heard,
Foxy's howls as he de-prickled his tail.

THE HUSKY AND THE BOBCAT

There was a little husky
Who one day went exploring,
And there upon an Arctic rock
He found a bobcat snoring.

Ah! A quaint little pussycat,
I'll make that feline jump,
And as the husky snarled and barked
A great big paw went thump.

You see bobcats are no ordinary cat
They're tough and rather mean,
They eat huskies for their lunch
On toast with margarine.

The husky turned, the bobcat chased,
The canine was so scared,
Dog hair flew onto the snow
As the bobcat's claws were bared.

The husky found a hollow log,
Shelter, safe at last,
The bobcat far too big to fit,
Snarled and then went past.

FUNKY THE MONKEY

Funky the monkey
A cheeky little fellow,
Grabbed the lion's mane,
It made him roar and bellow.

He scampered up a tree
Where the lion couldn't climb,
He laughed and called, "Poor Leo,"
As he swung from vine to vine.

He grabbed a juicy leaf
From a giraffe about to eat,
Then ran down the tree
And tickled all his feet.

He swung on to a bull frog,
Knocked him from his lily-pad.
Funky gave a chuckle.
But the bull frog looked quite mad.

Funky climbed a tree again
And shook a coconut free,
It landed on a gorilla
Dining out for tea.

The gorilla yelled, "I'll get you,"
Funky laughed and shook his head,
But just then his vine broke
And to the ground he sped.

DIRT TRACK WALLY

"I'm Wally the wombat
And I like to take a ride,
On my souped-up skateboard
Through the countryside."

"My problem is I'm nocturnal
I can only ride at night,
And my souped-up skateboard
 Doesn't have a light."

"I'm whizzing through the bush,
Look out kangaroo!
If you don't get off this track
I'll make mince meat out of you."

"Move out the echidna,
You're spikes don't scare me,
I'm rough enough and tough enough
To pin you to a tree."

"I'm Wally the wombat
King of the bush dirt track."
But just then his skateboard slipped
And Wally went kasplat!

THE WITCH'S BIRTHDAY ZOO

She was dressed in mauve, a pointed hat,
She stirred the cauldron round,
She was chanting words unknown,
It was a very eerie sound.

Her face was white and wrinkled,
There was a wart upon her nose,
She sprinkled magic powder in
Then petals from a rose.

She tapped the cauldron with her wand
Then out sprang a kangaroo,
He was followed by his bush friends
Wombat, lizard, koala, to name a few.

The magic wand was playing music
A party had begun,
Kanga started jumping
He was having so much fun.

Koala stripped the willow,
Wombat waddled from side to side,
Witchy upon her magic broom
Around the room did ride.

You see it was the witch's birthday,
And witch's friends are very few,
So she cast a spell to make some guests
To come to her birthday zoo.

ATTACK OF THE GIANT DINOSAUR

I didn't really mean
To do what I had done,
I trod on a dinosaur's tail
And now I'm on the run.

He's about fourteen metres long
And he's breathing down my neck,
My heart is purely throbbing
And my nerves are all a wreck.

He's just about on top of me
His teeth about to crunch,
Oh where do you hide from a dinosaur
When you're about to be his lunch.

"Stop playing with that lizard Tommy
And come on in for tea,"
"Ah, you'd spoil any game mum
For a little boy like me."

KING OF THE JUNGLE

I'm Leo the mighty lion
So strong and very proud,
There's no other animal in the jungle
That can ever make me cowered.
I strut along with my flowing mane,
It gives me a royal look,
The other animals walk around
Daren't stare or I'll cut them down,
Oh I'm Leo the mighty lion,
So fierce and very proud.

I'm king of the jungle so people say
And I think I would have to agree,
For I have never seen another animal
That can wear a crown like me.
When my roar is heard throughout the jungle
All other animals turn and run in fright,
For my roar has just announced
That the king is coming into sight.

One day a crocodile said to me
From you I'll take a bite,
But when he heard my mighty roar
His scales dropped off in fright.

A handbag I did make of him
And to this very day,
From the lesson of the crocodile
No animal doth have their say.

GHOSTS

I don't know why ghosts
Are so troublesome at times,
They seem to get their fun from
Making dogs howl and whine.
To scare the pants off people
And to make them run with fright,
Oh why, oh why do ghosts
Go into a frenzy of a night?
They think they're kind of smart
When they sneak right up on you,
And make your hair stand on end!
Oh they drive me round the bend,
Although, sometimes I wish I was a ghost,
I might do the same things too.

IMAGINATION

While walking in the woods one day
I saw a funny little mouse,
He squeaked to me, "Come follow me,"
He led me to a chocolate house.
Lime juice flowed along gutters
Made of musk and licorice strips,
Marhmallow curtains hung on curtain rods
Attached to creamy caramel whips.
We drank and ate for an hour long,
The chocolate house slowly disappeared,
Then the mouse gave an enormous squeak,
He vanished, how very weird.
Well, I've been back to those woods
Many times, looking for that mouse,
Perhaps he exploded from eating too much,
Perhaps, there was never a chocolate house.

TYRANNOSAURUS REX

Tyrannosaurus Rex is a name that's hard to say,
You won't see him any more because he's long had his day,
He roamed the ancient lands before man was ever born,
He arrived soon after the world first saw its dawn.
He stood six metres high, fourteen metres in length,
He ate other animals and had tremendous strength,
He used his teeth to rip and his tail for a rudder,
When he moved around the ground would really shudder.
Although his brain was small he was still very bold,
But when the weather changed he suffered from the cold,
And when the landscape changed to form new mountain ranges,
Alas no more TR, he was not adaptable to changes.

THE BOA WAS A GOER

I was on safari in the jungle
With my mate called Wrong-way Jack,
After being lost for several days
We decided to turn back,
As we journeyed 'long a jungle path
Wrong-way Jack let out a gasp,
I turned my head to see a snake
Had him firmly in his grasp.

Jack's eyes began bulging, his false teeth popped out,
A boa-constrictor had him firmly held,
His tongue jutted out from his squirming face,
"I'll save you Jack," I yelled.

I unravelled that snake, hard work it was,
He just didn't want to let go,
But finally he relented and took for the trees,
Jack's breath was beginning to flow.

As Jack got up with his teeth in his hand
He began to get white with rage,
"I'm going to catch you, you rotten snake,
On that I'll bet a year's wage."

Well Jack took off in hot pursuit
Of that hissing and loathsome snake,
He yelled as he ran through the jungle palms,
"From your skin a belt I'll make."

GRANDMA'S FALSE TEETH

Grandma Strong from Kurrajong
Wore a set of false teeth,
Each night she'd take them out
To give her mouth relief.
 She'd put them in some water
To keep them nice and clean,
When she woke she'd brush them
And put them back where they'd been.
 However this night it was very cold,
Her teeth froze in the water,
Still the same when morning came
The ice had really caught her.
 She couldn't do her shopping,
She couldn't talk on the phone,
She had to wait for the teeth to thaw
Before she left her home.

TREE-HOUSE HARRY

Harry sits in his tree-house
Eating jungle grapes,
He's feared throughout the jungle,
He's known as king of the apes.
 When a call goes out for help
Then Harry will be there,
Leopard cloth and tiger thongs,
It really makes you stare.
You can hear Harry yelling
As he swings from tree to tree,
It's usually when he's falling,
He's no Tarzan you see.
 His reputation gained
When an ape he fell upon,
Now the animals run for cover
When Harry comes along.

SPELLBOUND

The witch's broom
Went vroom vroom
As she rode across the sky,
Her pointed hat
And robes of black
Played shadows on the high.
She cast a spell
And when it fell
It landed right on me,
Now there's no joy
For this little boy
I eat worms up in a tree.

SPACENAUT

It came and hovered over me,
So shiny, large and round,
A humming sound, a beam of light
It took me off the ground.
I was on board a flying saucer
With ultra-sounds and cosmic light,
It was full of blue Venusians
I trembled from the fright.
The leader of the aliens said,
"Would you like to take a trip?
Around the stars and planets
In our sonic fast spaceship."
I saw the rings of Saturn,
Jupiter's moons stood out so bright,
I felt the coldness of Pluto
As we raced throughout the night.
 We rode upon the Big Dipper,
At the Milky Way we quenched our thirst,
Then headed back for Earth
Through the mighty universe.
 The next thing I remember
Was my mum waking me in bed,
She said, "Your eyes look starry,"
I just nodded my weary head.

KEY INTO BOOKS

One day while I was sitting
In the playground eating lunch,
I dropped my tabouli salad,
It made an awful crunch.
I picked my salad up,
A magic key was underneath,
It said, "Take me to the library,"
I did with disbelief.
I dashed into the library,
The key pulled me to a shelf,
It made the books fly open
To expose a literary wealth.
It really was a magic key,
You see Pirate Pete had come alive,
He was chasing Ollie Octopus
Around the fiction side.
I hid behind the non-fiction
Then Bass and Flinders rowed on by,
They yelled, "Where's the water?'
But I said, " The library's dry."
I slowly gathered courage,
I realised they wouldn't harm,
Books are full of information
And their characters full of charm.
I started feeling sleepy,
Then someone started pushing me,
My teacher woke me up
In the playground near a tree.
The next time in the library
The magic key I didn't need,
To be thoroughly entertained,
I only had to read.

PIRATA PETE

My name is Pirate Pete and I'm captain of the ship,
I keep my men in order with the power of my whip,
With a cutlass by my side and a parrot on my shoulder,
I roam the seven seas, there is no other bolder.
I fly the Jolly Roger, merchant ships I route and plunder,
There's never been a ship afloat that can put this pirate under,
I wear a patch on one eye and I have a wooden leg,
And when I'm feeling thirsty I drink rum from my keg.
I've captured ships, stole their gold, made people walk the plank,
And with my trusty cannon their ships I always sank,
But there comes a day where a pirate can be a buccaneer no more,
You see my leg has now got wood-worm and I can't make it to the shore.

A CROOK COOK

Captain Cook he had a chook
But eggs it wouldn't lay,
So he ate the chook and now he's crook,
He cockle-doodle-doos all day.
Captain Cook he had a horse
But the horse it wouldn't run,
So he ate the horse as a main course
Now he neighs in the noon day sun.
Captain Cook he had a cat
But the cat it wouldn't meow,
So he ate the cat, now he's so fat,
His belly-button just went pow!

BANDITO THE MEXICAN CAT

Bandito, the Mexican cat,
Was counting pesos where he sat,
A sneaky cat, you never knew
Exactly what he was going to do.
 Stealthily working in the night,
Stealing jewels kept out of sight,
A nimble safe cracker of renown,
Robbing mansions all over town.
 A black cat only rarely seen,
People only knowing where he'd been,
Rich townsfolk lived in dreaded fear
Of the whiskered feline coming near.
 Bandito, the dangerous Mexican cat,
Not the kind you'd want to pat,
But that won't happen cause you won't see
As he goes about, his crime spree.
 A royal maharaja visiting old Mexico
Saw his rubies disappear so,
Not a track, just merely a trace,
Of a few cat hairs out of place.
 So many good citizens were upset,
Police finally hatched a plan to be set,
Eventually this feline of criminal ilk,
Was brought down by, a large bowl of milk.

Wheelie Bin Fun

Our wheelie bin gives me a grin,
When I put my brother in,
I push him hard from the rear,
He yells out loud, "No rubbish here,"
We really love our wheelie bin.

 But recently from the top of a hill,
I pushed him off for a thrill,
He took off at break-neck speed,
It really was a dirty deed,
He now wears plaster from the spill.

 No more wheelie bins for us,
My brother still is oozing pus,
And when he hears the nightly din
Of a garbage truck and a wheelie bin,
He goes ballistic—what a fuss.

MUSICAL DILEMMA

An exuberant orchestra fellow,
Over exerted the stroke on his cello,
His bow flew like a spear
Zooming into a posh lady's ear,
The recital was stopped by her bellow.

An opera scout looking on,
Heard the posh lady's bellowing song,
He signed her up to appear
So the whole world could hear,
Now she sings for an operatic throng.

PHONE BONE DELIGHT

A dog on a phone
Rang, 'Dial-a-Bone,'
He wanted a delivery
Made to his home.

 He also asked for
Small liver treats,
There's nothing like dining
On two meats.

He smacked his lips
And howled at the moon,
Anticipating the delivery
Would be there soon.

When the van arrived
He tuckered in,
Growling and chomping
With his toothy grin.

 Ah, there's nothing like
Having a phone,
When I'm feeling peckish
I dial a bone.

SILKY MILKY

My pet cat looks so fat,
He's always drinking milk,
He says he only drinks so much
So his hair shines like silk.
Personally I think he's fibbing,
I think he's just a greedy cat,
If he'd only reduce his intake,
He'd still look shiny, but not so fat.

WITCHY POO FROM DUNEDOO

I'm Witchy Poo from Dunedoo,
I'm a flaming outback witch,
You won't see me rounding cattle up
Or digging in a ditch,
 I like to cast spells
Just like those other city witches do,
I've cast so many spells out back,
Successful ones too.
 Did you know that emus
Always used to fly,
That is until that nasty bird,
Well….dropped one in my eye.
So I cast a spell
So they could only move along the ground,
No more zooming through the air for them,
They're terra firma bound.
 And as for those walking kangaroos,
Too many gathered near my shack,
So I cast a spell of hiccups
Just to get them back.
 But my most successful spell of all,
And there certainly is no doubt,
Was when I took the rain away
And created all this drought.
 There's only one more thing to tell you,
And it's how I got my name,
The locals gave it to me,
Just after the emu took its aim.

SIPPING SODA

I love sipping soda
Through a coloured straw,
Your lips must be puckered
As you make the draw,
It may get quite noisy
At the bottom of the glass,
But make sure there's nothing left
As you make your final pass.

FRESH BREAD AND HONEY

Tap, tap, tap, with my feet,
I'm tapping out a pathway beat,
Clunk, clunk, clunk, with my money,
I just bought some bread and honey.
Home I go from the store,
I can't wait to pour, pour, pour,
With the honey, spread, spread, spread,
It's so tasty on fresh bread.

LEAPING LEANA

They called her Leaping Leana,
She was famous through the land,
It started when she jumped a cattle dog
Then a woolly lamb,
Next she jumped a wheelbarrow,
Then she jumped a car,
Her fame was spreading everywhere
Through shearing shed and far.
Next she jumped a wagon,
Without a second thought,
Then she jumped a brahma bull
When the wild beast was caught.
But alas her career came to an end,
When her eyesight started to go,
She jumped right over a cliff
Thinking there was water down below.

THE NEW FARM ANIMAL

Camellia Rose blew her nose,
The noise was quite gigantic,
Elouise Goose flapped her wings,
Other animals acting frantic.
 Betsy Dog ducked in her kennel
As the din echoed round the farm,
It sounded like a foghorn
And was causing such alarm.
 Neddy Horse hid in his stall,
Clara Cow inside the milking shed,
The pigs no longer at their trough
Waiting to be fed.
 When the sound finally disappeared
Camellia Rose spoke in a voice so calm,
" I'm just a llama with a cold,
No one will come to harm."

SAILOR BILL AND THE PELICAN

Sailor Bill decided to sail
Around the world where others had failed,
With him his trusted right-hand man,
Cedric, the pelican.

Cedric would give him plenty of warning
When the seas looked like storming,
He'd flap his wings and do some squawking
Just like the pelican was talking.

When there was no food at the table,
This smart bird was very able
To fly from the ship and catch some fish,
Then serve them up in Sailor Bill's dish.

Alas the pair were known well
At ports of call where the ocean swell,
They always seemed to be having fun,
Sailor Bill and his crew of one.

SNEEZE

I wonder what causes it ?
That thing they call a sneeze,
It comes rushing out your mouth
As easy as you please,
There seldom is a warning
Just a great big noise,
It makes any gasping kid
Really lose his poise.

NOISY ANIMALS

Grunt, grunt, grunt, bray, bray, bray,
I couldn't get my nap today,
Cluck, cluck, cluck, bark, bark, bark,
I shut my eyes when it was dark,
But– moo, moo, moo, bleat, bleat, bleat,
How does this farmer get to sleep?
I know, I'll put some ear plugs in,
Snore, snore, snore, grin, grin, grin.

ROLLER SKATING MOUSE

A roller skating mouse
Rudely came into my house,
He stuck his tongue out
As he went racing by,
He was taking all my cheese
As easy as you please,
It just made me want to cry.
So I went to a pet store
And paid just a little more
To buy a roller-skating cat,
When I took him to my house
He caught that rolling mouse,
Now I can eat my cheesy snack.

THE MEAT PIE EATER

A young boy ate ten pies,
Now on the ground he sadly lies,
His face is green, his mouth is red,
From where all the sauce has spread.
His mother warned him not to eat
Beyond capacity for a treat,
His stomach rumbles once again,
Next time he'll try one less than ten.

LUMPY RUMPY

Lumpy Rumpy a rather large lad,
Had a reputation for being so bad,
He rolled a mega barrel down the hill,
Full of dead fish and the content spill.
The reeking aroma made people sad,
With pegs on their noses they got so mad,
The townspeople chased Lumpy down the street,
When they catch him they'll paddle his seat.

LOVE IN THE SWAMP

A young green frog
Strumming on a log,
His warbling sounds
Singing words of love.
Strumming and crooning
He warbled long,
About the moon and stars,
In his lovebird song.
He also sung about
His wetlands home,
Singing and a plucking
On his swampy roam.

Taken in by the sounds
Of this sweet melody,
Another green frog
Swaying in her tree.
Love arrows bounced
Between the two,
The pounding of their hearts
Just grew and grew.
Now they sit together
On a leafy lily-pad,
He sings songs
About being a dad.

THE GIANT HAT

Wacko Jack from Ballarat
Built the most enormous hat,
Made of canvas with a great big brim,
Three storeys tall with a velvet trim.
Some dogs howled, while babies cried
When they saw Jack's hat worn with pride,
Old ladies gulped, while others grinned,
Until one day a howling wind
Saw Jack take off, up he went,
Sailing high like a flying tent,
He yelled out loud with a face so grim,
"Next time I'll make a smaller brim."

That same night when it was late,
A UFO spotted above Bass Strait,
But it was only Jack still holding on
To the flying hat that'd gone so wrong.

ALIEN DANGER

Granger was in danger
An alien landed in his yard,
So he slimed him with his slime-gun,
The alien running hard.

He jumped into his rocket ship
And pulled the portals down,
He blasted into space
With a great big alien frown.

Granger told his parents,
They just laughed and shook their heads,
That is until they saw the scorch marks,
Just near the old chook sheds.

FARMYARD BAND

The cow was playing cowbells,
Giddy Goat joined in on his guitar,
The horse was hoofing bongo drums,
Animals started coming from afar.
The chicken clucked an egg out,
Pig was oinking right in time,
Duck was tinkling on her triangle
While dog was hammering on his chime.
Pussy picked up her piccolo,
Goose was flapping on his flute,
Donkey brayed on a big trombone,
It really was a farmyard hoot.

CAT-ASTROPHIC

Out on the prowl with a vicious growl
There's no purr-fect 'bout me,
I'm a striking, strutting tom-cat,
Flying fur, a specialty.
Don't come near, my pretty dear,
I'm a rogue so independent,
With sharpened claws I explore
So viciously resplendent.
I roam the ally and dilly dally
Finding food foolishly dispatched,
I fill my belly with gluttony,
From garbage bins not latched.
Once before when a labrador
Came near one starless night,
My growl much bigger than he mustered
He quickly slunk from sight.
 So if one day you accidentally stray
To the ally where I roam,
My prowling stealth could affect your health
As you make your dash for home.

ROO-BOY

Between the spinifex and gibber, across the dry, hot sand,
Lenny sits as proud as punch with leather straps in hand,
His roo it has a saddle and a bit between its teeth,
When he wants to change direction, he gives the reins a reef.
You see Lenny rides a kanga, a great big bounding roo,
The locals think he's crazy as he comes bouncing through,
From Coolah to Walgett, Burke, Gunnedah and Broken Hill,
You'll hear the call as Roo-boy passes, "You're a flaming dill."
But Lenny sits as pleased as punch, crunching spinifex,
Under the paws of the red roo, that he christened Rex,
The mulga bush and salt pan is where the unlikely pair roam,
The never-never, back of beyond, the outback is their home.
From White Cliffs to Wilcannia you'll hear the walloping sound,
The great big thump beyond Black Stump racing cross the ground,
The dingoes and galahs, the corellas join in too,
Laughing at their loudest as the pair come jumping through.
But one day opinions changed in the town of Coober Pedy,
Arriving were some robbers, dangerous and so greedy,
Roo-boy bounced the villains into the crusty ground,
The locals called him hero, an outback legend found.
Now when Roo-boy's seen; that is where the story's spread,
Jackaroos and Jillaroos dip the akubra hats upon their head,
They pay homage to the boy that saved the outback town,
The place where inhabitants spend most time underground.
Now a song's just been written; Roo-boy is its name,
It's spread across Australia, giving the pair such fame,
But you won't see them in a fancy place, being kept and well fed,
They still sleep under stars, using dried tussocks for a bed.

THE FOX

Predatory, crafty, stealthily stepping,
Creeping shadow in the night,
Lanky, villainous and shifty,
Trying to keep out of sight.
Silhouette cast in the moonlight,
Red hair shimmering so,
He's sneaking around for dinner,
Whispering wind is on the blow.
Chook-house is approaching,
Salivating lips slap up and down,
Now crawling on his belly,
Across the dew-drenched ground.
Clambering up the boarded side,
Suddenly a loud barking noise,
A scampering fox darts back to the bush
Displaying such little poise.

TEAM SPIRIT

I asked the cricket coach
If I could play in the First Grade Team,
He said that just couldn't happen,
It was only in my dream.
I said what about if the whole team got sick,
Would I stand a chance then?
He shook his head from side to side,
And crossed my name off with his pen.
Well, I guess, I better tell you coach,
Ah, you know that stew that I brought in,
I suggest the team don't eat it,
If they want a chance to win.
But alas, the warning came too late,
The team had already tuckered down,
They got a lot of runs that day,
Just not on the cricket ground.

THE MONSTER

The monster stood glaring at the door
I stood trembling with my feet stuck to the floor,
He was green and slimy and his face was a mess,
Oh could it be the monster from Loch Ness?
As I looked at him and he looked at me
I wished I was a bird up in a tree,
I' d rather be anywhere than eye to eye
With a monster that looks like a dropped Big Ben Pie.
My knees began knocking, my voice in a mutter,
Slowly but surely I started to stutter,
"If you've come to get me I'll give you a fight,"
But within a moment he was gone from my sight.
What a relief as I lay back in my chair,
Embarrassed by my reflection,
It was all that was there.

LITTLE BICYCLE

I rode my little bicycle
Down the little street,
I pushed my little pedals
With my little feet,
When my little bicycle
Hit a great big bump,
I flew over the handle-bars
And landed with a thump.
I pushed my little bicycle
Home to see my mum,
She put some little band-aids on
Where I needed some.
Now I'm all patched up,
But my little handle-bars are bent,
I'm sure my dad can fix them
After my little accident.

WHERE IS HE?

A young scientist from Madrid,
Suddenly fell off the grid,
Developing a new vanishing cream
With powers extreme,
Everyone wondered where he was hid.

HOT DOGS

I like a little yellow,
Mixed in with my red,
I like my sauce and mustard
Squeezed on to my bread,
I like my bread in a roll
With a frankfurt sticking out,
I really love my hot dogs,
They're cuisine to rave about.

DOG TALES

My flipping, flopping, bounding dog,
Excitedly jumped over a fallen log,
He should have looked before he leapt,
Landing in a creek with his misstep,
Now he's dog paddling past a frog.

PROFESSOR DOGARATI

Professor Dogarati was a smarty,
An inventor of renown,
His creations for his canine friends
Well known all over town.
He made a soft warming pad,
For those little pups just born,
He made battery heated jackets;
Many in winter being worn.
He invented a musical collar,
Worn by dogs on their daily stroll,
Many a mutt tapping out a tune
In time to rock and roll.
 But his best invention of them all
Was an automatic dispensing machine,
Distributing timely doggy treats
Made up of a la carte cuisine.

Noisy Horse

A horse of course
Can find the source
To whinny with
Such great force,
This force of course
Can make him hoarse,
He just may suffer
Equine remorse.

ROLLY– POLLY PLATYPUS

"Rolly-polly platypus
Where did you get that bill?"
"I got it from a quacking duck,
He left it in his will."
"Rolly-polly platypus
Where did you get those claws?"
"A lion gave them to me
From his great big paws."
"Rolly- polly platypus
Where did you get that fur?"
"A koala gave it to me
Said the colour wasn't her."
"Rolly-polly platypus
Where did you get those flippers?"
"I bought them from K-Mart,
They make such dandy slippers."

PELICAN

A pelican tellican
Where the fish all are,
A pelican catchican
Fishes near and far.
With a giant scoopican
Dive upon the pond,
With his giant beakican
Store then for later on.

Grizzly Bear

Are you aware that a Grizzly Bear
Is tall and very powerful,
Don't disturb him while he naps
Or you might get a growl full.
If you see him in a forest,
Then seek shelter from a tree,
Make sure your scent is downwind
Or you just might be his tea.

www.ingramcontent.com/pod-product-compliance
Lightning Source LLC
LaVergne TN
LVHW052321210726
843527LV00031B/491